Sometimes being with the right person changes our life in a beautiful way. To my loving parents who supported my dreams; my dear sister, who supported me in every step and my best friend, who makes every day brighter. Thank you for being my inspiration and guiding light. You have made me believe in hope, aspiration, resilience, inner strength, small steps and hard work.

FROM DISTRACTION TO DESTINATION THROUGH NATURE

MEENA PANNEERSELVAM

Made with ♥ on the Notion Press Platform
www.notionpress.com

Contents

Contents

Preface

Life is like nature, full of struggles and growth. Just as a rainbow appears after the rain, dreams emerge after life's challenges. Like a butterfly emerging from its cocoon, we grow stronger after facing difficulties. Small moments of confidence, like fireflies lighting the night, guide us through dark times. And like a crane soaring through the sky, our ambition can lift us toward our greatest dreams. These poems explore the parallel between the struggles found in nature and those we face in our own lives while pursuing our passions. Each verse reflects the perseverance, resilience and strength required to push forward, even when the path ahead seems impossible. As Stephen Hawking rightly said, "However difficult life may seem, there is always something you can do and succeed at. It matters that you don't just give up".

When faced with the toughest challenges, remember, "Impossible? I am possible". Your determination and will power can turn any dream into reality. Through these thirty poems, I invite you to witness nature's raw power and grace, finding inspiration to navigate your own struggles. May these words remind you that, like the seasons, the rainbow or the light that rises after the darkest night, your dreams are within reach – if you have the courage to keep moving forward. Never give up.

If this book helps even one person in their journey toward achieving their passion, my purpose in writing this book will be fulfilled.I hope that as you read these poems, you find something that resonates with you. Perhaps they will offer a new perspective on your own struggles while pursuing your dreams. I am grateful to share these poems with you, and I hope they bring you comfort, joy, and a deeper connection to the world around you.

The path to success is not easy, it's filled with obstacles and stones along the way. But one must not change their path due to fear of obstacles or stones. Whether your passion feels small or big, it's the effort you put into it that determines whether it becomes a reality or not.

Keep

pushing forward.

CARVE YOUR PATH

Oh, beautiful stone,

In the hands of the Sculptor,

You are becoming a beautiful statue.

Oh, beautiful stone,

In the hands of Earth,

You are becoming a precious diamond.

Oh, beautiful stone,

In the hands of Early Humans,

You are becoming a powerful weapon.

Oh, beautiful stone,

In the hands of the Engineer,

You are becoming a charming house.

Oh, beautiful stone,

In the hands of a devotee,

You are becoming a deity.

Oh, beautiful stone,

In the hands of Sea,

You are becoming smooth pebbles.

Oh, beautiful stone,

In the hands of Engraver,

You are becoming an inscription.

Oh, beautiful stone,

In the hands of the physiotherapist,

You are managing pain and tension.

One small stone can make big difference.

Like stone we too,

Have our own individual identity.

Amidst the chaos

In today's fast paced world,

We forget our own identity.

Discover your identity,

Carve your path,

Bring your vision to life.

Unfurl your wing,

Be fearless and step forward,

To stand out from the crowd.

THROUGH TRUST, WE RISE

Pleasant smell resides within a tiny flower

Delicious sweetness resides within honey

Hope resides within a butterfly's emergence

Patience resides within a tortoise shell

Courage resides within a lion's heart

Determination resides within an ant's trail

Resilience resides within a camel's journey

Creativity resides within a potter's wheel

Resourcefulness resides within a rat

Beauty resides within a peacock.

Calmness resides within a cow

Freedom resides within an eagle

Trust creates an exemplary system

Foundation of every success,

is trust that resides within us.

There is a champion within everyone

Trust that new heights will always be reached

Every record is meant to be broken.

With consistency and hard work,

We can achieve the Impossible.

There's always an opportunity to enhance,

There will be no success,

Until you accept the pain of discipline

Trust yourself to make a big difference.

The day when you experience that deep love for your passion run towards it. No matter how much it hurts or tests you never lose your courage.

Never stop striving

For

what sets your soul on fire.

PATH TO GREATNESS

Cocoa beans are roasted

to get the flavour and texture

which turns them

into a delicious chocolate.

Sugarcane is crushed

to extract its juice

which turns them

into a granulated sugar.

Carbon is subjected

to immense pressure and heat

which turns them

into a valuable diamond.

Seed is planted

to germinate and sprout

which turns them

into a blooming flower.

Milk is curdled

to get thicker and lumps

which turns them

into a creamy cheese.

Corn is heated

to release moisture into the kernel

which turns them

into a popcorn.

Sand is heated

to extremely high temperatures

which turns them

into a glass.

Stone is mined

to get cut and polished

which turns them

into a marble.

Clay is moulded

to get fired in a kiln

which turns them

into a beautiful pottery.

Gold is mined

to get melted and shaped

which turns them

into a jewellery.

In order to become,

the best version of yourself

sometimes we have to

go through tough times.

So, if you ever felt like crushed,

stuck in the darkness or under pressure,

it doesn't mean you're failing,

you're prepared to become your better version.

Your struggles preparing you to a new level,

Pressure turns you into a stronger person,

Darkness reveals your true potential,

Remember dark holds no terror.

If you face hard times don't fear them,

Rather trust the process,

keep marching ahead

they transform you into a powerful person.

MOVING FORWARD

Be like a river

that always

moves forward.

Be like a sun

that always

rise and shine.

Be like an ocean

that always

embrace change.

Be like a rain

that always

nurture what they touch.

Be like an eagle

that always

soar above the storm.

Be like a dawn

that always

start each day fresh.

Be like a star

that always

shines in the darkest times.

Believe there is something inside you

Greater than any obstacle.

Remind yourself

that it's okay not to be perfect.

Never let your dreams

remain just dreams.

Focus on progress, not perfection.

BE A STAR

When the sun goes down,

Beneath the evening's soft embrace,

The moon takes over the sky

Casting a silvery glow

across the landscape.

Stars begin to twinkle

Each unique in their own way

They are shimmering jewels

which are scattered across

the night sky like a diamond.

Moon takes the spotlight,

but stars don't compete

with the moon.

They simply shine

in their own way.

Moonlight may seem brighter,

but the stars still shine.

Stars stay true and persistent

in its path without

worrying about the spotlight.

Keep shining in your own way

No matter how much small

Your light seems to shine.

Presence of moon doesn't

Stop stars from shining.

Similarly, we have to

continue our journey.

No matter how much

failure we face in our life,

Still find your way to glow.

Regardless of the

Challenges we face

Always believe in persistence.

Remember stars shines the brightest

when its darkest.

Be a star in your sky.

Your brilliance is

Never dimmed by

Anyone else's light.

BE YOURSELF.

THE JOY OF THE ORDINARY

Sound of birds chirping

in the early dawn.

Soft whisper of the

ocean waves at sunrise.

A piece of music that

brings back beautiful memories.

Fragrance of fresh

flowers in a garden.

The rustle of leaves

in the wind.

The joy of reading a

good book in the morning.

A handwritten letter

from someone special

in this technology driven world.

First bite taste of a

favourite childhood candy.

Pleasant smell of

raindrop on dry earth.

Simple beauty of an

old photograph.

Beauty of a warm sunrays

after a week's storm.

Aroma of coffee

in the early morning.

The morning fragrance of

incense sticks burning.

Writing our name in

first page of a new notebook.

Clock ticking sound

in the silent afternoon.

The way grass sway

gently in the breeze.

The way moonlight reflects

on a still lake amid darkness.

Gentle glow of fireflies

dancing in the night.

Beauty of a window corner

seat in a train.

Beauty of catching falling

leaves from a tree.

Beauty of gazing at

cloud shapes in the sky.

Light that's getting through

the veins of the leaves.

Life can be chaotic,

Filled with pressures of work

and responsibilities but

in these busy times

these small things

offer stability and help us

to reconnect with ourselves

and the world around us.

These tiny things though

seems to be insignificant

in comparing with the

grand things of life

but fills us with

awe and gratitude.

They help us to

slow down and

Savor life

rather than rushing through it.

When we learn to celebrate

the simple moments

we become more content

with our lives as they are.

Extraordinary is seeing

Beauty in the ordinary.

Not looking

actually seeing.

Because life is not to be

enjoyed but to be CELEBRATED.

Difficulties in life are meant

to make us better, not bitter.

Difficult roads often lead to beautiful

destinations we never dreamed of.

It's never easy,

but sure, it will be Worth it.

EMERGENCE OF BEAUTY

Rainbows appears in the sky,

After a rainstorm.

They remind us that

Even in difficult times

If we stay calm and hopeful,

We can witness the

Emergence of beauty and peace.

Just like rainbow's vibrant spectrum.

Without rain, there would be

No Rainbows in the sky.

Without challenges, there would be

No growth in our life.

Challenges are meant to be challenged.

Rainbows will disappear quickly,

reminds us beautiful moments

are temporary and make

the most of each passing moment.

Rainbows doesn't form instantly,

It takes time to form.

Best things take time and patience

Which leads us towards the goal.

So, enjoy the process.

There's negativity around

Be strong enough to choose positive.

Focus on doing your best.

Definitely you will succeed.

Don't be afraid of storm

Because it gives us the

Vibrant colours of rainbows.

Sometimes hardships and challenges

Makes us stronger than we think.

Valor – be courageous,

Innovative -think from a new perspective,

Bold – take risks with confidence,

Growth – learn from failures and mistakes,

Yearn – stay curious to pursue your passion,

Optimism – focus on solutions not on problems,

Resilience – bounce back stronger than ever.

FACE YOUR PROBLEMS

The struggle of getting out of

the cocoon was so necessary

for the butterfly's growth.

Without pushing its fluid from

its stomach to its wings

it can't fly.

Even though it's painful

It struggles to push it out.

Otherwise, it would remain

Crippled forever.

The butterfly begins to emerge

struggling hard to tear

its home after many weeks.

A little caterpillar slowly

metamorphoses into a butterfly.

Just like the caterpillar sheds

its old skin to become a butterfly,

sometimes we have to accept

and embrace change.

Because the change lies within us.

This transition doesn't happen overnight

It takes many days. Similarly,

our growth also takes some time,

and it will be so colourful one day.

It faces so many challenges

during its life cycle.

But it never gives up.

And yet it persists to

become its best version.

Butterflies are admired for

their simple yet stunning beauty.

Once butterflies emerge from

its cocoon they are free

to fly in its own paths.

Butterflies remind us

growth, transformation, and

pain are part and parcel of life.

We all have the ability

To flourish and reinvent

Ourselves after difficult stages.

Rise above every obstacle,

Have relentless courage to

conquer your fear.

Because every challenge is

a stepping stone and

every setback is a lesson.

Keep pushing forward

Because the path to Greatness

is paved with Perseverance and resilience.

Greatness awaits beyond barriers.

Pain changes people

but

people can change the pain,

use

your pain as a catalyst for

your personal growth

and transformation.

Pain is a comma not a full stop.

Some stones are meant to create pathways,

not

obstacles.

SHAPED BY THE STRUGGLE

In order to create an idol,

a sculptor doesn't add

anything new to it;

He simply removes

the excess.

Sometimes, we have to

strip away

distractions and naysayers

to discover our true potential.

The sculptor took his tools

and began chiseling the stone.

The stone, which is silent

and enduring the pain,

eventually transformed into

a beautiful idol.

It reminds us that

life is not easy to live, and

no one becomes great

Without struggle.

Even a stone is not shaped

into an idol unless it

is struck by a hammer.

Whenever you feel pain

and trouble in your life,

understand that these

hardships will bring

change and transformation.

POWER OF WORDS

Words can heal us,

Words can wound us.

Words can hurt us,

Words can console us.

Words can build us up,

Words can tear us down.

Words can encourage us,

Words can belittle us.

Words can unite us,

Words can divide us.

Words can bring clarity,

Words can confuse us.

Words can create peace,

Words can stir conflict.

Words can bring joy,

Words can bring sorrow.

Words can bring hope,

Words can bring despair.

Words can build trust,

Words can break trust.

Words can bring laughter,

Words can bring tears.

Words can spark creativity,

Words can suppress ideas.

Words can bring peace of mind,

Words can create anxiety.

Words can give us strength,

Words can make us weak.

Words can create bonds,

Words can create distance.

So, choose your words wisely,

Because they hold POWER.

Don't shy away from difficulties;

instead,

embrace them as your allies

and move forward.

FEAR ENDS WHEN HOPE ENTERS

When the sun sets,

we know that

it will rise again.

When the leaves fall,

we know that

they will grow back.

When the night comes,

we know that

The dawn will follow.

When a flower wilts,

we know that

it will bloom once again.

When the moon hides,

we know that

It will appear again.

When the seasons change,

we know that

it's part of the cycle.

When the tide recedes,

we know that

it will return.

When life gets tough,

we should remember that

there is light at the end of the tunnel.

Always believe that

the road may be hard,

but the end will be worth it.

RUN YOUR OWN RACE

For some, the ocean is a destroyer.

For some, the ocean is a protector.

For some, the ocean is a guardian.

For some, the ocean is a threat.

The Ocean doesn't care,

What people think,

What people say,

What people criticize,

It simply reminds us,

To keep going with our purpose.

The people of the world will always

put some kind of label on us.

Be unaware of the labels

That people put on us.

If we pay attention to

what people are saying,

We will never succeed in our life.

Don't fight with time,

it's just a moment that changes.

One moment it moves, one moment it stops,

one moment it turns.

This journey of time is such that it tests your determination on the path to your goals.

Be the person who refuses to quit.

Nothing comes easy.

HOPE NEVER DIES

The ant carries the granules of sugar,
Lays them up to the heights of the wall.
It falls, slips many times,
but still tries again.

The confidence in its mind
Stirs courage in its nerves.
It soars and slips,
Again, it rises,
Succeeds finally,
And takes its food home.

It reminds us the goal we dream of,

from far away,

looks beautiful and enticing.

But the path to conquer

is never as easy as it seems.

Thorns on the path

may test you,

but plucking out the thorns

and relishing those challenges

makes you strong from inside.

The hurdles might even

break you from inside,

the slips and falls

on the way will demoralize you

and make you feel weak.

But the journey worth the effort.

Every bit of a journey is a joy.

The only thing standing

between you and your goal

is your effort and positive mindset.

Make sure to move ahead

and never look back.

Work on the solution,

instead of the problem.

Work hard and keep

trying till you succeed.

So do not stop until

THE SKY TOUCHES THE LAND.

STRENGTH IN PATIENCE

A beautiful crane

stands on one leg

in a lake,

carefully watching the water.

It lets the small fish

pass by, but catches

the big ones,

feasting on them.

The crane waits silently,

For the right moment to strike.

Similarly, in life,

With patience and focus,

we too find the

Right opportunity to shine.

The Crane's unwavering focus,

During hunting teaches us

The importance of clarity and concentration

in achieving our dreams.

Cranes migrate

Thousands of miles,

Able to adjust to new

Environments and situations.

They teach us that

the ability to adapt to

changing circumstances

is crucial for survival and success.

Like a crane,

we must elevate,

Ourselves above adversity

To gain a clearer perspective.

The elegance of a crane in flight

Reminds us that patience and perseverance

Lead us to great heights.

In the moments of uncertainty,

It walks gracefully on land

And soars high in the sky.

Similarly, we must find

Stability even in turbulent times.

Trust that every end is the

Foundation of a new beginning.

And struggle is a part of the journey

Towards victory.

When you are determined to reach
your goal,

however

Difficult the path may be,
your burning passion

Drive you forward towards your goal.
Real failure is

The failure to try.

Your only limit is you.

Break free from your own limitations.

BE UNSTOPPABLE

Fireflies don't follow the light;

they generate their own light

and dispel the darkness

around them.

Similarly, your passion

doesn't follow beliefs; it

becomes the belief system itself

and dispels the darkness of your life.

If you truly want to achieve

your dreams,

you will find a way.

You will stop at nothing to reach them.

Winners don't allow

pain to stop them.

They use it as

fuel to push harder than ever.

Every challenge, every setback,

every pain is an opportunity

to learn, to grow and become

even more UNSTOPPABLE.

DETERMINATION MAKES DIAMONDS

A diamond is just a stone,

But no other stone

is as precious as this one.

It doesn't just bring happiness,

but also requires many sacrifices.

The sparkle of this diamond

is not achieved

without many struggles.

Its brilliance is forged

in the fire of adversity.

It teaches us that

Valuable things in life

often comes with

Challenges and struggles

But the end result is worth it.

In life, we all reach points,

where we have to choose

between giving up or

going all in.

In those moments

we must remember

how many times we have been

knocked down

you have this

wild potential inside you,

just like a diamond.

Every monumental achievement

that's ever been done,

was once thought impossible.

But the people who went

after their dreams,

MADE IT POSSIBLE.

On the path to

pursuing your passion

each pain and

struggle you face

is acceptable

as long as you don't give up.

One step at a time will help you
reach your destination.
Don't leave everything to fate or
compare yourself to others.
It won't solve your problems; instead,
it will create new ones.
Every fruit in the world has a unique taste,
and
no single fruit encompasses all flavour.

SUCCESS TAKES TIME

Success is like planting a tree.

You plant the seed,

you water it,

you give it sunlight,

and then you wait for it to grow.

It takes time for

the roots to flourish.

While waiting,

we keep nurturing it.

We don't give up on it

just because we don't see results.

We water the plant daily,

but we only get the fruit

at the right time.

No matter how hard

we work for the fruit,

it will take time.

That's how we need to

deal with our passion.

Plant them, nurture them

and give them time to grow.

Growth is a process

It doesn't happen overnight.

Success takes time.

EMBRACE CHANGE

Spring teaches us

the joy of new beginnings

and the promise of growth.

Summer teaches us

to live in the present moment

and cherish our freedom.

Autumn teaches us

how beautiful it is

to let things go.

Winter teaches us

to find strength

even in difficult times.

Patience and resilience -

after every winter

comes a new spring.

Embrace change.

Sometimes, a single hope

is all it takes to keep

you from giving up.

Reset, Breathe and Restart.

Search your goal from heart.

With faith make it as your identity.

Have faith in yourself,

your abilities and your decisions.

Because you only know

the value of your dream.

Every difficult situation becomes easy,

every destination achievable

and certainly, victory is yours.

STRENGTH LIES IN ADVERSITY

We can achieve

so many things in life,

just like how we

can write so many

things with a pencil.

When we write,

we guide the pencil

on how and where to write

we should not forget

that there is always

someone behind us,

pushing us to

move forward in life.

When we write with a pencil,

it becomes dull, and

we need to sharpen it.

While sharpening,

the pencil may face some pain,

but after its sharpened,

it writes even more beautiful.

Similarly, in life,

when we face difficulties or pain,

it actually makes us stronger.

We always have the option

to erase when we

write with a pencil.

Similarly, in life,

When we make mistakes,

We always have a chance to

Correct them.

Learn from your mistakes

and don't repeat them.

No matter how the pencil

looks from the outside,

its real beauty lies

in the lead, which writes.

Similarly, our physical appearance

don't matter as much as

our inner beauty.

How we look on the outside

Doesn't define us;

our inner beauty does.

Eventually, the life of a pencil

comes to an end,

but until that time,

it uses its lead

to the fullest.

Similarly, we must

make use of every second

to do good for ourselves and others

because life doesn't

offer second chances.

A pencil writes until

its lead is empty. Similarly,

we should never accept defeat.

we must face our problems

and give our 100%

to overcome them,

just like the pencil does.

HOLD YOUR DREAMS

If someone

holds your hand,

it will last

only for

a few minutes or hours.

It gives you a

temporary comfort

to reach your dreams.

But if you

hold your hand

you develop self-reliance,

resilience and confidence

and it will

last forever and ever.

You are the one

to decide whether to

hold on or let go.

Believe in yourself,

take the leap and

don't let fear

hold you back.

Dream, Believe and Achieve.

Sometimes, you just have

to follow your dreams

and trust your heart.

Believe what your heart tells you,
not what others say.

Naysayers are like advertisements –
just skip them to enjoy the show.

HAVE COURAGE IN THE DARKEST TIMES

Light and darkness share

an age-old relationship.

Every night has a dawn,

but the darkness just before

dawn is the deepest.

This profound darkness

only leads the night

towards the light.

Neither night can change its nature,

nor can darkness alter its fate.

When we face

darkest phases of our life,

we can't see hope, confidence or enthusiasm.

We become confused and lose hope.

At that time, remind yourself

that as dark as

the night may be,

your upcoming dawn will be equally bright.

With good guidance

during this phase of our life,

we can persevere.

Soon we learn

how to find our way

,even in the darkest times

and emerge victorious.

One second can't

change your life,

but the decision you

make in one second

can change your entire life.

That's why, in life,

think carefully before

making any decision.

No goal in this world

is bigger than

a person's courage.

DON'T BE AFRAID OF CHANGE

An eagle lives for 70 years.

After 40 years, its beak, body

and wings become heavy.

It then lies down in a place

and refuses food.

When they realize their body

has grown weak

they smash their beak

against a rock, causing injury.

Once the wound heals

They are able to live for

many more years.

But they must endure

the pain to achieve this.

Our future lies in our present.

The effort we put in today

Determines our future.

Sometimes we need to

let go of the fear of failure

and unpleasant old memories.

In order to embark a

new journey ahead,

we must release

our limiting beliefs.

When it rains,

all birds go to shelter.

But the eagle avoids rain by

flying above the clouds.

Problems in achieving

our goals are common to all.

But the attitude toward

solving them makes the difference.

When fear grips you down,

first it snatches away the door of

self-trust from you.

Never allow it to do so.

Because behind that door lies

your love for your passion.

In your victory over fear,

lies the defeat of your passion.

Never let your fear decide your fate.

NEVER LET YOUR FLAME FADE

When we place a lamp

in a windy place,

the flame of the lamp

wavers and may

even extinguished.

But if you place the lamp

in a windless place,

it will glow

emanating a great shine,

illuminating its surroundings.

Your dreams are like a flame,

fragile yet powerful.

Protect your spark by

surrounding yourself with positivity.

Remember even in windy conditions,

the flame can be rekindled.

Don't give up on your dreams

when faced with obstacles or setbacks.

Just as the lamp illuminates its surroundings

pursuing your dreams will light up your

path and guide you to your purpose.

Be resilient, adapt to challenges,

and never let your flame fade.

INVISIBLE YET IMPACTFUL

Salt makes our food tasty,

but it remains hidden,

not visible in the dish.

Even though salt is invisible,

its flavour remains.

Your unique talents

and perspectives can

leave a lasting impression

even if you are not

always in the spotlight.

To enhance the flavour of a preparation,

the salt dissolves and

gives up its identity.

To achieve greatness,

be willing to

dissolve your fear

and let go of your doubts.

Go ahead,

flavour the world

with your awesomeness!

Achieve all your goals.

Sometimes you will win,
sometimes you will learn,
but
never accept your defeat.

Just because it's taking time
doesn't mean it's not happening.

FOCUS ON YOUR PATH, NOT THE NOISE

A kite soars high in the sky,

but strong winds blow against it.

The kite doesn't fall or

get distracted by the wind.

It keeps soaring,

focussing on its flight.

While pursuing our goal,

some people try to demotivate us,

discourage us, pause very

disappointing comments on us.

But we should not lose our motivation.

We should continue our

work with a humble mindset.

We should ignore other's comments,

not out of arrogance or pride,

but simply to avoid getting

discouraged in pursuit of our goal.

UNLEASH YOUR INNER POTENTIAL

A musk deer wandered

through the forest,

captivated by a sweet fragrance.

Curious about the scent's origin

it searched far and wide,

but couldn't find the source.

The deer didn't know that,

the fragrance emanated

from its own body.

The musk deer's journey

teaches us that sometimes,

the answers we seek are

within us all along.

The musk deer's search for

the fragrance reminds us that
our worth and value come
from within, not from outside.
Trust your inner potential.
You have the power to
create the life you desire.
Stop searching outside and
start believing in yourself.

When the footsteps of your effort

grow weary,

let the wings of your dream

carry you towards your
destination.

How you see yourself matters.

You matter.

Losing anything is acceptable,

except yourself.

LEARN TO RISE

Woodpeckers keep pecking

away at trees,

no matter how tough the bark is.

They don't give up

after a few attempts;

they keep at it

until they succeed.

They teach us

the importance of perseverance

and sticking with our goals,

even when things get tough.

We all face obstacles

and challenges in life

that seem insurmountable.

There will be times

we feel like giving up

when the weight of our struggles

feels too heavy to bear.

The woodpecker reminds us to

keep going, to persist,

despite the odds.

Each small step,

each effort, brings us

closer to our goals,

no matter how distant they may seem.

The woodpecker doesn't strike randomly.

It carefully selects its target and

pecs with precision, ensuring

each strike counts.

It teaches us the value of

strategy and planning

in our endeavours.

When you face challenges

while pursuing your goals

Remember woodpeckers unwavering

spirit that reminds us

we all have an inner strength,

and we can overcome any obstacle

with determination and resilience.

Don't let setbacks defeat you,

Use them as opportunities to

Learn, grow and come back stronger.

Setbacks are temporary,

Comebacks are permanent.

THE POWER OF A SMILE

"Smile" -- just five letters.

The human signature.

Smile, and it will make your day,

As well as others'.

A smile can

lift you up,

build confidence,

warm your heart,

and bring joy to your life.

A smile won't make your troubles,

or anybody else's, disappear,

but it will make them

feel good about themselves

in a beautiful way.

Smile,

a beacon of hope

that makes everything beautiful.

Let your smile shine,

even in the darkest moments.

Smile through the struggles,

for better days will come.

Don't let crises

Steal your smile.

A mirror reflects beauty when whole,

but

when broken,

it becomes a weapon that harms us.

Stay focused and clear.
A fragmented mind can hurt your progress.

Keep your goals intact

and

let your passion reflect your true
strength.

PROTECT YOUR INNER PEACE

Just like a tortoise

withdraws its limbs

into its shell at

the sight of an obstacle,

we too must learn to

protect ourselves from

distractions and negative influences on

our journey toward our goal.

Whenever we face an

unfavourable situations,

whether it's an unhealthy temptation,

harmful gossip, or

discouraging words –

we must have the wisdom to

withdraw, refocus and

stay true to our purpose.

By guarding our senses and

remaining steadfast, we can

stay on the path to success,

keeping our minds clear,

our spirits strong,

and our goals in sight.

The tortoise reminds us that,

in the face of any challenge,

we must protect our inner peace

and keep moving forward

toward the life we envision.

Positive words empower people,

but unnecessary fault-finding

disempowers, discourages, and

weakens one's determination.

So, lets encourage people

with our positive words, and

not demotivate them

with unnecessary fault finding.

LESSONS FROM NATURE: RISING WITH PURPOSE

Every Sunrise reminds us

that each day holds new opportunities.

Every Sunset assures us

that tomorrow brings fresh beginnings.

White clouds gather,

painting a masterpiece in the sky.

The stars of midnight, like dreams,

illuminate the darkness above.

Birds flap their wings,

pushing forward with purpose.

Trees stand tall,

offering strength and resilience.

The buzzing of bees reminds us

that hard work brings sweet rewards.

Cows and sheep gaze peacefully,

grounded in the present moment.

Petals of blown roses flutter to the earth,

teaching us to embrace change.

Paddy crops dance in the wind,

showing us how to stay adaptable.

Water cascades down from distant peaks,

carving its own path with persistence.

Nature creates its own harmony,

teaching us that effort and patience bring beauty.

Today, we fail to notice

the Sunrise and the Sunset.

No longer pausing to

hear the birds' songs.

But there was a time when

We revelled in the

simplicity of nature's rhythm,

when children played in open fields

and adults found peace in nature's embrace.

Those days of chasing butterflies

taught us the joy of pursuing dreams.

Building mud piles reminded us

that great things start with small steps.

Jumping in puddles was a reminder

to embrace life's challenges.

Playing with trees was a call

to stay rooted in our values.

Nature nurtures our minds and bodies.

Yet in the rush of modern life,

we forget its power.

We drift further from it, damaging it

with every passing moment.

But why can't we change this?

Let's take a step forward and

look to nature for guidance.

Just as the sun rises, we too

can rise with new determination.

Just as the trees stand tall,

we can root ourselves in our goals.

Nature offers the most powerful lessons

in perseverance, growth and renewal.

So, let us embrace nature with open arms.

In its beauty and simplicity,

We can find strength, inspiration

and peace we need to pursue our dreams.

Nature is not just a place of rest,

but a constant reminder:

The comeback is always

greater than a setback.

Take the next chance to rise again

like a PHOENIX from the ashes.

www.ingramcontent.com/pod-product-compliance
Lightning Source LLC
LaVergne TN
LVHW041108150826
845673LV00007B/1966

* 9 7 9 8 8 9 7 4 4 5 0 9 7 *